Contents

PREVIEW

Alzheimer's is the most common cause of dementia among older adults. Dementia is the loss of cognitive functioning—thinking, remembering, and reasoning—and behavioral abilities to such an extent that it interferes with a person's daily life and activities. Dementia ranges in severity from the mildest stage, when it is just beginning to affect a person's functioning, to the most severe stage, when the person must depend completely on others for basic activities of daily living.

ALZHEIMER'S DIET RECIPES

BREAKFAST

1. Sweet and Spicy Tofu and Jalapeno Pad Thai

Total Time: 40 min

Prep Time: 15 min

Cook Time: 25 min

Servings: 6 (1 cup each)

Ingredients

- 1 tablespoon peanut oil
- 2 garlic cloves, minced
- 1 small jalapeno, seeds and membranes removed, minced
- 1/2 cup mushrooms, sliced
- 1 package tofu, drained and cut into cubes
- 1 package pad thai rice noodles
- 1/4 cup lime juice
- 1/4 cup low-sodium soy sauce
- 1 tablespoon honey

- pinch chipotle crushed red pepper
- 1/2 cup peanuts, coarsely chopped
- 1/2 cup carrots, shredded
- 2 tablespoons cilantro

Instructions

1. On the stovetop over medium-high heat, place a wok or deep saucepan and add oil, garlic, peppers, mushrooms, and tofu. Saute until tofu is browning and vegetables are softened.
2. Prepare noodles according to package instructions. Add cooked noodles to the wok or pan with the tofu and vegetable mixture.
3. In a small bowl, whisk together lime juice, soy sauce, honey, and crushed pepper. Pour over the tofu and vegetables. Mix together while still over the heat. Remove when thoroughly heated.
4. Divide noodle dish among six bowls. Top each with a sprinkle of peanuts, carrots, and cilantro, if desired.

2. Homemade Vegetarian Lo Mein

Total Time: 25 min

Prep Time: 10 min

Cook Time: 15 min

Servings: 4 (1 cup each)

Ingredients

- 2 brown rice and millet ramen cakes
- 2 tablespoons low-sodium soy sauce
- 2 tablespoons sesame oil
- 2 tablespoons agave nectar
- 1 tablespoon raw, unpasteurized apple cider vinegar
- 1 tablespoon fresh ginger, peeled and diced
- 1 teaspoon Sriracha (hot chili pepper sauce) (optional)
- 2 cups stir-fry vegetable mixture (snow peas, carrots, bell peppers, onions, broccoli, and cabbage)
- 4 ounces firm tofu, patted dry and cut into cubes

Instructions

1. Prepare the ramen noodles according to the directions on the package.
2. In a small bowl, whisk together soy sauce, oil, agave nectar, vinegar, ginger, and Sriracha, if using. Add vegetables and tofu to a different large bowl. Pour sauce on top and toss until well-coated
3. Add vegetable and tofu mixture on the stovetop over medium-high heat in a large wok or skillet. Cover and heat for 10 minutes, stirring occasionally. When vegetables begin to soften, it's ready.
4. Add noodles to the vegetable mixture and lightly toss. Remove from stove and serve while still warm.

3. Pan-Seared Salmon with Mediterranean Quinoa

Total Time: 35 min

Prep Time: 20 min

Cook Time: 15 min

Servings: 2

Ingredients

- 1/4 cup black olives
- 1/4 cup sun dried tomatoes
- 1/4 cup fresh parsley
- 1 clove garlic
- 1/2 cup quinoa, dry
- 1/2 pound (8 ounces) wild Alaskan salmon, raw
- 1/8 teaspoon black pepper
- 4 cups baby spinach
- 1 tablespoon olive oil
- 1/4 teaspoon dried basil
- 1/8 teaspoon salt
- 1 ounce feta cheese

Instructions

1. Chop olives, sun-dried tomatoes, and parsley. Peel and mince garlic clove. Set aside.

2. Cook quinoa according to package directions.

3. While the quinoa is cooking, pat your salmon dry with a paper towel. Rub each piece (cut in 2 if you have one large piece) with a small amount of olive oil and sprinkle with black pepper.

4. Heat a pan to medium-high heat. Once hot, add the salmon skin side up. Cook for three minutes, and then flip over and cook for three more minutes.

5. While the quinoa and salmon are cooking, heat your olive oil and garlic over medium heat in a separate pan. Once hot, add the baby spinach and sauté for a few minutes until it's wilted.

6. When your quinoa is done, mix in olives, sun-dried tomatoes, parsley, basil, and salt. Mix feta cheese in last.

7. Serve quinoa and spinach side by side with the salmon over the top. Enjoy!

4. Simple Vegetarian Spinach Lasagna

Total Time: 65 min

Prep Time: 20 min

Cook Time: 45 min

Servings: 9 (1 cup each)

Ingredients

- 1 package no-boil lasagna noodles
- 2 28-ounce cans tomato sauce
- 1/8 teaspoon kosher salt
- 1 teaspoon oregano
- 2 cloves garlic, finely minced
- 1 15-ounce container part-skim ricotta cheese
- 1 cup part-skim mozzarella cheese, grated
- 3 cups raw baby spinach leaves

Instructions

1. Preheat the oven the 350 F.
2. On the stovetop over medium heat, pour the tomato sauce into a saucepan. Add salt, oregano, and garlic.

Bring to a light boil, lower the heat, and simmer for a few minutes. Stir occasionally.

3. On the bottom of a 9x13 pan put a layer of tomato sauce. Place a layer of noodles on top, covering the bottom of the pan. Spread ricotta cheese on top of the noodles, top with spinach, and sprinkle with mozzarella cheese and coat with a small ladle full of sauce. Repeat the layers until you get to the top of the pan. Sprinkle the final layer with mozzarella cheese.

4. Place in the oven and bake for 45 minutes or until bubbly and cheese is golden brown on top.

5. Remove from the oven and allow to cool for a 10 minutes before serving.

5. Creamy Vegetarian Pumpkin Cauliflower Soup Recipe

Total Time: 55 min

Prep Time: 10 min

Cook Time: 45 min

Servings: 18 (1/2 cup each)

Ingredients

- 1 tablespoon canola oil
- 1 medium yellow onion, diced
- 2 28-ounce cans pumpkin puree
- 1 medium head of cauliflower, cut into small florets
- 2 1/2 cups low-sodium vegetable broth
- 1 teaspoon salt
- 1 teaspoon black pepper
- 1/2 teaspoon ground cloves
- 1 teaspoon ground nutmeg
- 1 teaspoon fresh tarragon, chopped
- 2 1/2 cups low-fat (2% fat) milk
- 1 teaspoon lemon juice

Instructions

1. Place oil in a large stock pot on the stovetop over medium heat.

2. Add onions and allow to cook until translucent (about 5 minutes).

3. Add pumpkin and stir. Heat for 5 minutes.

4. Add cauliflower and broth; cover. Cook until the cauliflower begins to soften (about 15 minutes).

5. Stir in herbs and spices (salt through tarragon). Stir well and allow to cook for another 10 minutes.

6. Using an immersion (hand-held) blender, puree the mixture until smooth directly in the pot.

7. Once smooth, add milk and stir well. Add the lemon juice, give it a final stir, and serve hot.

6. Quick and Easy Egg McMuffin-Style Sandwich

Total Time: 10 min

Prep Time: 5 min

Cook Time: 5 min

Servings: 1

Ingredients

- 1 whole wheat English muffin, toasted
- cooking spray
- 2 large eggs, scrambled
- 1 teaspoon ground turmeric
- 1 teaspoon garlic powder
- 2 fresh basil leaves, sliced
- 1/8 teaspoon kosher salt
- 1/4 of a small avocado, sliced
- 1 thin slice beefsteak tomato

Instructions

1. Put each half of the English muffin in the toaster. Allow toasting until the edges are crisp and slightly browned.

2. In a small skillet on the stovetop over medium-low heat, apply a spritz of cooking spray. In a small bowl, scramble eggs with turmeric, garlic powder, basil, and salt. Pour into heated skillet. With a spatula, scramble the eggs until light and fluffy. Remove from heat.

3. Place the scramble on half of the toasted muffin. Top with avocado and tomato slices.

4. Top with the half of the muffin. Serve while warm.

7. Sesame Garlic String Bean Almondine

Total Time: 35 min

Prep Time: 10 min

Cook Time: 25 min

Servings: 4 (1/2 cup each)

Ingredients

- 1 tablespoon sesame oil
- 1 garlic clove, minced
- ¼ large white onion, minced
- 2 cups green beans, washed and trimmed
- ½ freshly squeezed lemon juice
- ¼ cup raw, slivered almonds
- A pinch of kosher salt

Instructions

1. In a medium saute pan over medium-low heat, add oil and garlic. Saute for a minute. Add onions and saute for another minute until onions become translucent and slightly browned around the edges.
2. Toss in the green beans. Mix, cover, and allow to cook for a few minutes. Stir occasionally and allow to cook and steam under the cover for a few more minutes.

3. Add lemon juice, almonds, and salt and mix while cooking. Saute until green beans begin to soften. Remove from heat. Toss and portion into serving bowls or plates.

8. Creamy Slaw and Veggie Wrap

Total Time: 7 min

Prep Time: 7 min

Cook Time: 0 min

Servings: 3

Ingredients

- 2 cups broccoli and carrot slaw
- ½ cup marinated artichoke hearts, chopped
- ½ cup black beans
- 3 to 4 sprigs fresh cilantro, coarsely chopped
- 1 tablespoon extra virgin olive oil
- 1 tablespoon balsamic vinegar
- 1 teaspoon Dijon mustard
- 2 tablespoons plain low-fat Greek yogurt
- Salt and pepper to taste
- 3 10-inch whole grain wrap

Instructions

1. In a medium bowl, add the slaw, artichokes, beans, and cilantro; gently mix until combined.

2. In a small bowl, whisk together oil, vinegar, mustard, yogurt, salt, and pepper. Pour over the slaw bean mixture. Toss together until well coated.

3. Lay the wraps out on a cutting board. Place ⅓ of the slaw on each of the wraps. Roll them up and serve. Enjoy!

9. Grilled Peach Avocado and Arugula Flatbread

Total Time: 18 min

Prep Time: 10 min

Cook Time: 8 min

Servings: 8

Ingredients

- 2 tablespoons extra-virgin olive oil
- 2 tablespoons balsamic vinegar
- 1 teaspoon Dijon mustard
- 1 dash of salt and black pepper
- 1 large ripe peach, washed and sliced
- 2 large whole grain flatbreads or naan bread
- 2 cups arugula, washed and dried
- ½ large ripe avocado, cut into small chunks
- 2 tablespoon grated parmesan cheese

Instructions

1. Preheat grill to 400F.
2. In a small bowl, whisk together oil, vinegar, mustard, salt, and pepper.
3. Brush vinaigrette dressing onto peach slices. Place them on the heated grill. Pull the top over the grill and

allow peaches to cook for 1 to 2 minutes. Flip over and cook for another minute. Remove from grill.

4. Place flatbread on the grill to heat for 30 seconds on each side. Remove from grill.

5. Spread arugula on each flatbread. Gently add grilled peaches and avocado chunks spaced evenly on top of each; sprinkle with parmesan cheese. Drizzle remaining vinaigrette on top and serve.

10. Smoky Baked Bean Medley

Total Time: 70 min

Prep Time: 10 min

Cook Time: 60 min

Servings: 6 (1/2 cup each)

Ingredients

- 2 15-ounce cans tri-bean blend (kidney, pinto and black beans), rinsed and drained
- 2 8-ounce cans tomato sauce
- 1 tablespoon extra-virgin olive oil
- 1 small shallot, minced
- 1 teaspoon smoked paprika
- ½ teaspoon garlic powder
- 1 tablespoon raw, unpasteurized apple cider vinegar
- 1 tablespoon honey

Instructions

1. Preheat oven to 350F.
2. Add beans and tomato sauce to an oven-safe bowl. Stir gently until combined.
3. On the stovetop over medium-low heat, add oil to a small skillet. Heat for 20 seconds; add shallots. Saute

for a few minutes until translucent. Remove from heat.

4. Add cooked shallots to bowl with beans and tomato sauce. Add in paprika, garlic powder, apple cider vinegar, and honey. Stir gently until combined.

5. Place in the oven. Bake for 30 minutes; check and stir. Bake for 15 to 30 minutes longer to allow the flavors to meld together. Remove from oven and serve.

LUNCH

11. Chorizo Cauliflower Frittata

Prep Time: 10-15 mins

Cook Time: 20-25 mins

Total Time: 30-40 mins

Yield: Serves 8

Ingredients

- 10 large eggs
- ½ cup Greek yogurt
- 1 ½ teaspoons coarse salt
- 1 teaspoon dried oregano leaves
- 1 teaspoon chili powder
- 1 teaspoon onion powder
- ½ teaspoon garlic powder
- ½ teaspoon ground black pepper
- 4 ounces ground chorizo
- 3 cups fresh baby spinach
- 2 cups steamed cauliflower florets
- ½ cup shredded pepperjack cheese
- ¼ cup fresh cilantro, chopped

Instructions

1. Preheat oven to 350 degrees.
2. In a large bowl, whisk together the eggs, Greek yogurt, salt, oregano, chili powder, onion powder, garlic and black pepper until thoroughly combined. Set aside.
3. Heat a large nonstick oven-safe skillet or stove top casserole dish to medium. Add the chorizo and cook 2-3 minutes, breaking up with a spatula, until browned. Stir in the spinach and cook 1-2 minutes or until wilted. Reduce the heat to medium-low.
4. Push the chorizo and spinach mixture aside in the skillet or casserole dish to coat with cooking spray. Add the egg mixture to the pan and gently stir to incorporate the chorizo and spinach. Evenly distribute the cauliflower florets among the egg mixture. Top with the pepperjack cheese and cilantro. Once the sides start to bubble up and cook, remove from the stove and place in the oven. Cook 15-20 minutes or until set. Let slightly cool, then slice into wedges and serve.

12. Carrot Apple Bread with Walnut Streusel

Prep Time: 15 min

Cook Time: 55 min

Total Time: 1 hr 10 min

Yield: 1 loaf

Ingredients

Bread

- 1 ¼ cups oat, whole wheat pastry, whole wheat or all-purpose flour
- ¼ cup almond flour
- 2 tablespoons ground flax seed
- 1 ½ teaspoons ground cinnamon
- ½ teaspoon ground nutmeg
- ¾ teaspoon baking powder
- ¾ teaspoon baking soda
- ½ teaspoon coarse salt
- 2 medium ripe bananas (about 1 cup)
- ½ cup dark brown sugar
- ¼ cup oil
- 2 large eggs
- 1 teaspoon pure vanilla extract
- 2 medium carrots, shredded (about 1 ½ cups)
- 1 medium apple, shredded or diced (about 1 ½ cups)

Streusel

- 3 tablespoons melted butter
- ½ cup old-fashioned rolled oats
- ½ cup chopped walnuts
- 2 tablespoons brown sugar
- ½ teaspoon ground cinnamon

Instructions

1. Preheat oven to 350 degrees. Grease a loaf pan with cooking spray. Set aside.
2. In a medium mixing bowl, whisk together oat flour, almond flour, flax seed, cinnamon, nutmeg, baking powder, baking soda and salt.
3. In another medium bowl, use a hand mixer to whisk together bananas, brown sugar and oil until fluffy. Whisk in egg, then vanilla extract until thoroughly combined. Slowly add dry ingredients to the banana mixture while whisking on medium speed, just until combined. Fold in shredded carrot and apple. Pour mixture into the loaf pan.
4. In a small bowl, whisk together streusel ingredients. Evenly coat top of bread batter with the streusel mixture. Bake for 50-55 minutes, until toothpick

inserted in the center comes out clean. Allow to cool, then slice and serve.

13. Chorizo & Hash Brown Egg Muffins

Prep Time: 10 min

Cook Time: 20 min

Total Time: 30 min

Yield: 12 muffins

Ingredients

- ½-pound ground chorizo
- 10 large eggs
- 1 medium bell pepper or 4 mini bell peppers, seeded and diced
- 1 cup shredded hash browns
- 1 cup shredded Mexican cheeses
- ½ cup fresh cilantro, chopped
- 1 teaspoon smoked paprika
- ¾ teaspoon coarse salt
- ½ teaspoon ground black pepper
- ½ teaspoon onion powder
- ½ teaspoon garlic powder
- ¼ teaspoon crushed red pepper flakes

Instructions

1. Preheat oven to 350 degrees. Grease a 12-cup muffin tin with cooking spray. Set aside.

2. Heat a medium skillet to medium-low heat. Add chorizo and sauté until browned, breaking the chorizo into small pieces as it cooks. Drain and place in a large bowl. Add the remaining ingredients and whisk or stir until thoroughly combined.

3. Use a measuring cup to scoop the mixture into the prepared muffin tin, filling almost to the top. Bake 16-18 minutes or until egg is just set.

14. Soft Batch Cookies

Prep Time: 10 mins
Cook Time: 12 mins
Total Time: 22 mins
Yield: 18 cookies 1x

Ingredients

Cookies:

- 2 cups old-fashioned rolled oats
- 1 cup whole wheat pastry flour (or whole wheat flour)
- ½ teaspoon baking soda
- ½ teaspoon coarse salt
- ½ teaspoon ground cinnamon
- ⅓ cup oil
- ½ cup brown sugar
- 2 large eggs
- ⅔ cup vanilla yogurt
- 2 teaspoons pure vanilla extract

Mix-Ins:

- 2–3 tablespoons dark chocolate chips + 2–3 tablespoons unsweetened coconut flakes
- ½ small banana, smashed + ¼ cup blueberries

- 2 tablespoons peanut butter + 2 tablespoons strawberry preserves

Instructions

1. Preheat oven to 350 degrees. Line a large baking sheet with parchment paper.
2. In a medium mixing bowl, whisk together oats, flour, baking soda, salt and cinnamon.
3. In another medium mixing bowl, whisk together oil and brown sugar, until fluffy. Whisk in eggs, until incorporated, then whisk in vanilla yogurt and vanilla extract. Pour dry ingredients into wet ingredients and whisk until just combined.
4. Fold in desired mix-ins. Scoop dough using a 2-inch cookie scoop, about 1-inch apart on the baking sheet. Bake 9-12 minutes. Allow to slightly cool.

15. Monte Cristo Sandwich

Prep Time: 5-10 mins

Cook Time: 10-15 mins

Total Time: 15-25 mins

Yield: Makes 4 sandwiches

Ingredients

- 8 slices whole grain raisin bread
- 16 slices black forest ham
- 4 slices muenster cheese
- ¼ cup apricot preserves + more for serving
- ½ cup milk
- 4 large eggs
- ¼ teaspoon ground nutmeg
- Pinch ground cloves
- Pinch coarse salt
- 3–4 tablespoons salted butter
- Powdered sugar (optional)

Instructions

1. Layer 4 slices of bread with honey ham, muenster and apricot preserves. Place remaining bread slices on top.
2. In a shallow dish, whisk together milk, eggs, nutmeg, cloves and salt until combined.

3. Heat one tablespoon butter in a nonstick skillet to medium heat. Dip one assembled sandwich in milk/egg mixture, then place in the hot skillet. Cook 3-4 minutes per side, until bread is golden brown and cheese is completely melted. Repeat this process with remaining butter and sandwiches.
4. Slice each sandwich into 4 squares and serve with extra apricot preserves and powdered sugar (optional).

16. Sourdough & Sausage Strata

Prep Time: 15 mins

Cook Time: 60 mins

Total Time: 75 mins

Yield: 12 Servings

Ingredients

- 1 tablespoon olive oil
- ½ medium yellow onion, peeled and diced
- 1-pound all-natural breakfast sausage
- 3 cups chopped kale or spinach (any green)
- 2 roasted red peppers, chopped (optional)
- 3 cloves garlic, peeled and minced
- 4-ounces Gruyere or gouda cheese, diced
- 10 large eggs
- 1 cup milk
- ⅔ cup plain Greek yogurt
- ½ teaspoon coarse salt
- ½ teaspoon ground black pepper
- ¼ teaspoon crushed red pepper flakes
- 1 loaf sourdough bread, cubed

Instructions

1. Preheat oven to 350 degrees. Coat a 13×9 baking dish with cooking spray. Set aside.

2. In a large skillet, heat olive oil to medium heat. Add onion and saute 3-4 minutes, until just starting to soften. Add breakfast sausage and cook, breaking up into pieces with a wooden spoon, until almost all browned, about 6-7 minutes. Stir in greens, roasted red pepper (optional) and garlic and saute another 2-3 minutes, until greens are wilted.

3. In an extra-large mixing bowl, whisk together eggs, milk, Greek yogurt, salt, black pepper and red pepper flakes. Add sourdough bread cubes, sausage mixture and diced cheese to the bowl and toss to combine. Transfer to the greased baking dish and spread out evenly.

4. Bake 45-60 minutes, until set and knife inserted into the center comes out clean. Slice and serve.

17. Hash Brown Waffles with Turkey Sausage Gravy

Prep Time: 10-15 mins

Cook Time: 10-15 mins

Total Time: 20-30 mins

Yield: Serves 4

Ingredients

Turkey Sausage Gravy:

- 1-pound ground turkey breakfast sausage
- 3 tablespoons all-purpose flour
- 1 ½–2 cups milk
- 1 teaspoon coarse salt
- 1 ground black pepper
- Crushed red pepper flakes, to taste (optional)

Hash Brown Waffles:

- 4 cups frozen shredded hash brown potatoes, thawed
- 2 large eggs
- ¼ cup shredded cheddar cheese
- ½ teaspoon coarse salt
- ¼ teaspoon ground black pepper
- ¼ teaspoon garlic powder

To Assemble:

- 4 over-easy eggs
- Handful of greens (sautéed or raw)

Instructions

1. Heat large skillet to medium-high heat. Add sausage and cook, breaking up with a wooden spoon, until browned, about 5-7 minutes. Stir in flour and cook for about a minute. Whisk in low fat milk and bring to a simmer until thickened, about 4-6 minutes, stirring regularly. Season with salt and pepper to taste and stir in crushed red pepper flakes, if desired.

2. Heat a waffle iron to medium-high heat. Coat generously with cooking spray. In a large mixing bowl, thoroughly combine hash browns, eggs, cheese, salt, pepper and garlic powder. Fill waffle iron with a layer of the hash brown mixture and close the lid. Cook 4-5 minutes, until hash brown is browned and crispy. Remove waffle with forks, then repeat the process with remaining hash brown mixture.

3. Top waffles with fried eggs, turkey sausage gravy and greens.

18. Caramelized Banana & Peanut Butter Oatmeal

Prep Time: 5 min

Cook Time: 10 min

Total Time: 15 min

Yield: Serves 6

Ingredients

- 3 ½–4 cups water
- 1 ½ cups old-fashioned rolled oats
- ½ cup chia seeds
- ½ tablespoon ground cinnamon
- 1 teaspoon pure vanilla extract
- ½ teaspoon coarse salt
- ½ cup natural peanut butter
- ½ cup milk of choice + more for serving
- 3 tablespoons pure maple syrup + more for serving
- 2 tablespoons butter
- 1 teaspoon brown sugar
- 3 yellow bananas, peeled and sliced
- ½ cup chopped walnuts and/or sliced almonds

Instructions

1. Bring water to a boil in a large saucepan. Pour oats and chia seeds into the water, bring to a boil, then reduce to a simmer for about 5 minutes, stirring frequently, until oats are soft. Remove from heat and stir in cinnamon, vanilla extract, salt, peanut butter, milk and maple syrup until combined.

2. In a medium skillet, melt butter and brown sugar at medium-high heat. Add sliced bananas and cook 1-2 minutes per side, until browned, flipping once.

3. Scoop oatmeal into bowls and top with milk and maple syrup, as desired, and walnuts/almonds and caramelized bananas.

19. Mexican Black Bean & Sweet Potato Skillet

Prep Time: 10 mins

Cook Time: 20 mins

Total Time: 30 mins

Yield: 4 Servings

Ingredients

- 1 tablespoon canola oil
- 2 bell peppers, sliced
- 2 tablespoons minced fresh garlic
- 1 (15-ounce) can low sodium black beans, rinsed and drained
- 2 cups cooked cubed sweet potatoes
- 1 tablespoon chili powder
- 1 teaspoon ground cumin
- Coarse salt and ground black pepper, to taste
- 4 Safest Choice™ pasteurized eggs
- 1 avocado, sliced
- 1 lime, wedged
- ¼ cup scallions, sliced
- Toasted corn tortillas, for serving

Instructions

1. Heat canola oil in a large cast iron or non-stick skillet to medium-high heat. Add bell peppers and saute 1-2 minutes. Add garlic and saute an additional 30 seconds. Add black beans, sweet potatoes, chili powder, cumin and a pinch of salt and pepper. Cook 2-3 minutes, stirring occasionally, until beans and sweet potatoes are hot.

2. Scoop hash onto 4 dinner plates. Heat skillet again to medium heat and coat with cooking spray. Crack eggs into the plate and season with a pinch of salt and pepper. Allow to cook until white starts to set, about 2 minutes. Turn skillet to low heat and cover with a lid. Cook an additional minute, just until the white is set on top but yolk is runny. Place cooked eggs on plated hash.

3. Garnish with avocado, lime wedges and scallions and serve with toasted corn tortillas.

20. Chicken and Black Bean Cilantro Lime Burrito

Total Time: 40 min

Prep Time: 10 min

Cook Time: 30 min

Servings: 6 (1 burrito each)

Ingredients

- 1 teaspoon cayenne pepper
- 1 teaspoon smoked paprika
- 1 teaspoon ground turmeric
- 1 teaspoon kosher salt
- 1 teaspoon black pepper
- 2 to 4 ounce skinless chicken breasts
- 1/2 cup apple cider vinegar
- 1/8 cup water
- 1 tablespoon low-sodium Worcestershire sauce
- 1 tablespoon tomato paste
- 1 tablespoon brown sugar
- 6 large spinach wraps
- ½ ripe avocado
- 1 15-ounce can black beans, drained and rinsed
- 1 cup shredded Romaine lettuce

- ½ cup chopped cherry tomatoes
- ¼ cup chopped cilantro leaves
- 1 medium lime, cut into six wedges

Instruction

1. Put cayenne, paprika, turmeric, salt and pepper in a medium bowl. Mix together and add chicken breasts. Coat on both sides.

2. Place chicken into the slow cooker/pressure cooker bowl. Add vinegar, water, Worcestershire sauce, tomato paste, sugar. (Alternative: bake chicken in the oven at 350 degrees for 30 to 40 minutes or until internal temperature reaches 165 degrees). Cook in slow or pressure cooker according the directions. Shred the chicken with two forks and place in a bowl with the sauce.

3. Place each tortilla in a skillet over medium heat for 30 to 60 seconds, until warm. Spread each one with a thin slice of avocado, covering the whole surface.

4. Fold the two sides into the center than pull the bottom half over the ingredients and tuck it under and cover

with the top half of the tortilla to make a tight burrito wrap.

5. Fold the two sides into the center than pull the bottom half over the ingredients and tuck it under and cover with the top half of the tortilla to make a tight burrito wrap.

DINNERS

Prep Time: 5-10 mins

Cook Time: 10-15 mins

Total Time: 15-25 mins

Yield: Serves 8

Ingredients

- 1 tablespoon olive oil
- 1-pound ground hot or mild Italian sausage
- 2 cloves garlic, peeled and minced
- 4–5 cups baby spinach
- 15-ounce can cannellini beans, drained and rinsed
- 2 teaspoons dried oregano leaves
- ½ teaspoon coarse salt
- ½ teaspoon freshly ground black pepper
- 2 (32-ounce) containers unsalted chicken stock
- 12-ounce bag fresh cheese tortellini
- Freshly shaved Parmesan cheese, for garnish

Instructions

1. Heat oil in a large Dutch oven or stock pot to medium heat. Add sausage and cook 4-5 minutes, until browned, breaking it up with a wooden spoon as it cooks.

2. Stir in the garlic and spinach and saute until spinach is wilted, about 2 minutes. Add cannellini beans, oregano, salt and pepper.

3. Add the stock to pot and bring to a simmer. Add tortellini and reduce heat to medium and allow to simmer, about 7-8 minutes, until tortellini is cooked. Taste and adjust seasoning, if necessary.

4. Serve in bowls and garnish with Parmesan cheese.

22. Sweet Corn & Zucchini Gnocchi Skillet

Prep Time: 10-15 mins

Cook Time: 15-20 mins

Total Time: 25-35 mins

Yield: Serves 6

Ingredients

- 1-pound whole grain gnocchi
- 2 tablespoons olive oil
- ½ medium yellow onion, peeled and diced
- 1 medium red bell pepper, stemmed and diced
- 4 ears sweet corn, cut from the cob
- 2 medium zucchinis, diced
- 4 cloves garlic, peeled and minced
- 3 tablespoons half and half
- Zest and juice of 1 medium lime (about 2 tablespoons)
- 1 ¼ teaspoons kosher or sea salt
- ½ teaspoon ground black pepper
- ½ cup freshly grated Parmesan cheese, divided
- ½ cup fresh basil leaves, chiffonade

Instructions

1. Bring a large stock pot of water to a boil. Add the gnocchi and cook 4-5 minutes or until the gnocchi float to the surface. Drain and set aside.

2. Heat the olive oil in a large skillet to medium. Add the onion, bell pepper and sweet corn and sauté 4-5 minutes or until soft. Stir in the gnocchi, zucchini and garlic and sauté 1-2 minutes or until gnocchi is lightly browned. Stir in the half and half, lime zest and juice, salt, black pepper, and half of the Parmesan cheese. Bring to a simmer for 2-3 minutes. Stir in half of the basil.

3. Serve gnocchi skillet in bowls and top with remaining Parmesan cheese and basil.

23. Carrot Fries with Chipotle Aioli

Prep Time: 10-15 mins

Cook Time: 15-20 mins

Total Time: 25-35 mins

Yield: Serves 6

Ingredients

Chipotle Aioli:

- 6 ounces plain Greek yogurt
- 2 tablespoons mayonnaise
- 2 chipotle chilies, finely chopped + 2 tablespoons adobo sauce
- Zest and juice of 1 lime
- 2 teaspoons chili powder
- 1 teaspoon honey
- Dash coarse salt and ground black pepper

Carrot Fries:

- 2 pounds carrots, cut into fry shape
- 1 tablespoon oil
- Dash coarse salt and ground black pepper
- 2 tablespoons fresh cilantro, chopped (optional)

Instructions

1. Preheat grill to medium-high heat or oven to 425 degrees.

2. To make aioli, whisk together yogurt, mayonnaise, chilies with adobo sauce, lime zest and juice, chili powder and honey. Season with salt and pepper; stir to combine. Taste and adjust seasoning, if necessary. Refrigerate until ready to use.

3. Drizzle carrots with oil and season with salt and pepper. Toss to coat. Place carrot fries on preheated grill against the grates, cooking for 15-20 minutes, turning regularly. Or, if you're making them in the oven, line on a baking sheet and roast 15-20 minutes. Remove carrot fries and drizzle with chipotle aioli and garnish with chopped cilantro.

23. Asparagus-Stuffed Chicken with Roasted Fingerling Potatoes

Prep Time: 10-15 mins

Cook Time: 20-25 mins

Total Time: 30-40 mins

Yield: Serves 4

Ingredients

- 4 slices uncured bacon, chopped
- 2 tablespoons olive oil, divided
- 4 (4-6 ounce) boneless skinless chicken breasts
- 1 ½ teaspoons Italian seasoning
- 1 teaspoon garlic powder
- ¾ teaspoon coarse salt, divided
- ½ teaspoon ground black pepper
- 12 spears asparagus, trimmed
- ¼ cup sliced Greek or kalamata olives (optional)
- 4 slices muenster, provolone or mozzarella cheese
- 1-pound fingerling potatoes, halved

Instructions

1. Preheat the oven to 400 degrees.

2. Heat a large oven-safe skillet or stove-top casserole dish to medium heat. Add the bacon and cook 8-10 minutes or until crispy, stirring occasionally. Use a slotted spoon to remove from the pan and place on a paper towel-lined plate. Set aside. Drain the bacon grease from the pan.

3. While the bacon cooks, cut a pocket into the side of each chicken breast, being careful not to cut all the way through. Season all sides of the chicken breast with Italian seasoning, garlic powder, ½ teaspoon salt and black pepper. Open the pocket of each chicken breast and tuck in a slice of cheese, 3 spears of asparagus, crumbled bacon and a spoonful of olives (if using).

4. Add 1 tablespoon of the olive oil to the same pan and bring to medium-high heat. Once hot, carefully add the stuffed chicken breasts and sear 3-4 minutes on the top side or until browned and crisp. Flip the chicken. Add the potatoes and toss with the remaining olive oil at the bottom of the pan. Season the potatoes with the remaining salt. Place the pan in the oven and cook 15-20 minutes or until the internal temperature

of the chicken reaches 165 degrees and the potatoes are just fork tender.

5. Remove from the oven and let rest 5 minutes. Remove the toothpicks. Serve.

24. Salmon Nicoise Salad

Prep Time: 10-15 mins

Cook Time: 6-10 mins

Total Time: 16-25 mins

Yield: Serves 6

Ingredients

Lemon Dressing:

- Zest and juice of 2 medium lemons
- 1 tablespoon Dijon mustard
- ½ tablespoon honey
- ⅓ cup olive oil
- ½ teaspoon coarse salt
- ¼ teaspoon ground black pepper

Niçoise Salad:

- ½ pound baby Yukon or red potatoes, halved
- 1-pound green beans, trimmed
- 6 cups butter lettuce
- 6 hard-boiled or soft-boiled eggs, halved
- 4 mini cucumbers or 1 medium English cucumber, sliced
- 1-pint cherry or grape tomatoes, halved
- ½ cup Greek or kalamata olives

Salmon:

- 1 tablespoon olive oil
- 1-pound fresh salmon, skin removed
- ½ teaspoon coarse salt
- ¼ teaspoon ground black pepper

Instructions

1. Bring a large pot of salted water to a boil.
2. In a small bowl, whisk together the lemon zest and juice, Dijon mustard, honey, olive oil, salt and black pepper. Taste and adjust seasoning, if necessary. Refrigerate until ready to use.
3. Add the potatoes to the boiling water and cook 5 minutes. Add the green beans and cook the potatoes and beans another 3-4 minutes. Transfer to a large bowl of ice water. Use a slotted spoon to transfer the potatoes and green beans to a paper towel-lined plate to dry.
4. Arrange salad bowls with butter lettuce, potatoes, green beans, eggs, cucumbers, tomatoes and olives. Set aside.
5. Heat the olive oil in a large nonstick skillet or cast-iron pan to medium heat. Season the salmon with salt

and black pepper. Once the pan is hot, add the salmon and cook 2-3 minutes per side or until it just starts to flake when gently pressed with the back of a fork. Let slightly cool, then transfer salmon pieces to the salad bowls.

6. Drizzle lemon dressing on each salad and serve immediately.

25. Cashew Chicken Lettuce Wraps

Prep Time: 10-15 mins

Cook Time: 10-15 mins

Total Time: 20-30 mins

Yield: Serves 6

Ingredients

Cashew Sauce:

- 6 tablespoons cashew, almond or peanut butter
- ¼ cup brown sugar
- ¼ cup low sodium soy sauce or tamari
- 3 tablespoons sesame oil
- 1 tablespoon Sriracha or chili garlic sauce
- Zest and juice of 2 medium limes
- 1-inch piece fresh ginger, peeled and minced
- Splash hot water

Chicken and Lettuce Wraps:

- 1 tablespoon oil
- 1–1 ½ pounds ground chicken
- 10 ounce bag coleslaw mix
- Coarse salt and ground black pepper, to taste
- 2 heads Boston lettuce (or Bibb)
- Handful fresh cilantro
- Handful chopped cashews

- Sriracha, to taste

Instructions

1. In a medium mixing bowl, whisk together cashew sauce ingredients until well incorporated. Set aside.

2. Heat oil to medium-high heat in a large skillet. Add chicken and cook 2-3 minutes. Stir in coleslaw mix and cook 5-6 minutes, until cabbage is wilted and chicken is fully cooked and browned. Season with a generous pinch of salt and pepper. Stir in cashew sauce and simmer 2-3 minutes, until thickened. Remove from heat.

3. Place lettuce cups on a plate. Spoon chicken mixture into each cup and garnish with cilantro, cashews and Sriracha.

26. Blackened Fish Tacos with Pico de Gallo

Prep Time: 10-15 mins

Cook Time: 5-10 mins

Total Time: 15-25 mins

Yield: Makes 8 tacos

Ingredients

Pico de Gallo:

- 2 medium ripe tomatoes, cored and diced
- ½ small white onion, peeled and minced
- ½ medium jalapeno, seeded and minced (optional)
- ¼ cup fresh cilantro, chopped
- Zest and juice of 2 medium limes
- ½ teaspoon kosher or sea salt

Fish Tacos:

- 1-pound white fish filets, skins removed
- 2 teaspoons oil
- 2 teaspoons blackened seasoning*
- ¼ cup plain Greek yogurt or sour cream
- Juice of ½ medium lime
- 8 corn tortillas, toasted
- 1 medium avocado, peeled, cored and sliced

Instructions

1. In a medium glass bowl, stir together the pico de gallo ingredients. Cover and refrigerate.
2. Heat a large non-stick skillet or grill to medium heat. Brush the fish filets with oil, then coat with blackened seasoning. Cook in the skillet or on the grill 2-3 minute per side or until fish flakes easily with a fork.
3. In a small bowl, stir together the yogurt and lime juice.
4. Serve fish on toasted corn tortillas with slices of avocado, pico de gallo and a drizzle of lime yogurt.

27. Cheesy Taco Pasta

Prep Time: 10-15 mins

Cook Time: 20-25 mins

Total Time: 30-40 mins

Yield: Serves 8

Ingredients

- 1-pound whole grain macaroni or shells
- 1 tablespoon oil
- ½ medium yellow onion, peeled and diced
- 1-pound lean ground beef, turkey or chicken
- 3–4 cloves garlic, peeled and minced
- 2 ½ tablespoons chili powder
- 1 tablespoon ground cumin
- 2 teaspoons smoked paprika
- 1 ¾ teaspoons coarse salt
- ½ teaspoon ground black pepper
- 15-ounce can black beans, rinsed and drained
- 15-ounce can fire roasted diced tomatoes
- ½ cup unsalted chicken, vegetable or beef stock
- ½ cup evaporated milk
- 1 ½ cups shredded cheddar cheese
- ½ cup fresh cilantro leaves, chopped

- Diced avocado, sour cream and crushed tortilla chips, for serving

Instructions

1. Bring a large pot of water to a boil. Cook pasta according to package directions. Drain and set aside.
2. In a large skillet or Dutch oven, heat oil to medium. Add the onion and sauté 3-4 minutes or until slightly soft. Add the ground beef and cook 7-8 minutes or until the beef is browned, breaking it up with a wooden spoon as it cooked. Stir in the garlic, chili powder, cumin, smoked paprika, salt and black pepper and sauté 30-60 seconds or until fragrant.
3. Add the black beans, tomatoes, stock and evaporated milk to the pot and bring to a simmer. Remove from the heat and stir in the cheddar cheese until melted. Add the pasta and cilantro and stir to combine. Taste and adjust seasoning, if necessary.
4. Serve taco pasta in bowls topped with avocado, sour cream and crushed tortilla chips.

28. Chicken Parmesan Pasta Bake

Prep Time: 10-15 mins

Cook Time: 20-25 mins

Total Time: 30-40 mins

Yield: Serves 8

Ingredients

- 1-pound whole grain tubular pasta
- 3 tablespoons olive oil
- 1-pound chicken breast, cubed
- 1 teaspoon Italian seasoning (optional)
- 1 ½ teaspoons kosher salt, divided
- ½ teaspoon ground black pepper, divided
- 4 cups fresh baby spinach or chopped kale
- 4–5 cloves garlic, peeled and minced
- 4 tablespoons all-purpose flour
- 3 cups unsalted chicken or vegetable stock
- 12-ounces evaporated milk
- 2 cups shredded Italian cheeses (mozzarella, provolone), divided
- ½ cup freshly shaved or grated parmesan cheese, divided

- ¼ cup flat-leaf Italian parsley, chopped

Instructions

1. Preheat oven to 375 degrees.
2. Bring a large pot of salted water to a boil. Cook pasta according to package directions. Drain and set aside.
3. Heat olive oil in a Dutch oven or large oven-safe pot. Add cubed chicken and season with the Italian seasoing (if using), ½ teaspoon salt and ¼ teaspoon pepper. Cook, stirring occasionally, until chicken is opaque. Add spinach/kale and saute 2-3 minutes, until mostly wilted. Add garlic and saute 30-60 seconds, until fragrant. Stir in the flour.
4. Pour in the stock and evaporated milk and bring to a simmer, stirring frequently, for 5-6 minutes or until thickened. Season with the remaining salt and pepper. Add the 1 ½ cups of the shredded Italian cheese and ¼ cup of the Parmesan cheese until melted. Taste and adjust the seasoning, if necessary. Fold in the cooked pasta until combined.
5. Sprinkle the remaining shredded Italian cheeses and Parmesan cheese on the top of the pasta. Bake 10-15 minutes or until melted and bubbly. Optional: Broil 2-

3 minutes or until cheese is lightly browned. Let slightly cool, then serve topped with chopped parsley.

29. Cauliflower Alfredo Sauce

Prep Time: 10-15 mins

Cook Time: 10-15 mins

Total Time: 20-30 mins

Yield: Serves 6

Ingredients

- 9-ounces fresh fettuccine or linguine*
- 3 cups cooked cauliflower florets
- ½ cup evaporated milk
- ¼ cup unsalted vegetable stock
- Zest and juice of ½ medium lemon
- 1 ¾ teaspoons kosher or sea salt
- ½ teaspoon freshly ground black pepper
- Pinch freshly ground nutmeg
- Pinch cayenne pepper
- 3 tablespoons butter
- 2 tablespoons extra-virgin olive oil
- 4 cloves garlic, peeled and minced
- ½ cup freshly grated Parmesan cheese
- ¼ cup flat-leaf Italian parsley, chopped

Instructions

1. Bring a large pot of salted water to a boil. Cook the pasta according to package directions. Drain and set aside.

2. Place cauliflower, milk, stock, lemon, salt, black pepper, nutmeg and cayenne pepper in a blender and puree until smooth.

3. Heat the butter and olive oil in a large skillet to medium-low heat. Add the garlic and sauté 30-60 seconds or until fragrant. Pour the cauliflower puree into the skillet and bring to a simmer. Stir in the Parmesan cheese until melted. Taste and adjust seasoning, if necessary. Add the cooked pasta and toss to coat.

4. Serve in bowls and garnish with chopped parsley.

30. Spaghetti Pie

Prep Time: 10-15 mins

Cook Time: 40-45 mins

Total Time: 50-60 mins

Yield: Serves 8

Ingredients

- ½-pound whole grain spaghetti
- 1 tablespoon olive oil
- ½-pound natural turkey or pork Italian sausage (or ground beef, chicken or turkey)
- 3–4 cups fresh spinach, chopped
- 4–5 cloves garlic, minced
- 1 tablespoon Italian seasoning
- ¼ teaspoon crushed red pepper flakes
- 1 (24-ounce) jar marinara
- ½ cup cottage cheese
- 2 tablespoon basil pesto
- 2 large eggs
- ½ teaspoon coarse salt
- ½ teaspoon ground black pepper
- 1 cup shredded mozzarella cheese
- ¼ cup freshly grated Parmesan
- ¼ cup flat-leaf Italian parsley, chopped (optional)

Instructions

1. Preheat the oven to 350 degrees.

2. Bring a large pot of water to a boil. Cook pasta according to package directions. Drain and set aside.

3. In a Dutch oven or stove-top casserole dish, heat olive oil to medium. Add the sausage and sauté 5-7 minutes or until lightly browned and cooked through, breaking into small pieces as you sauté. Add the spinach and garlic and sauté another 2-3 minutes or until the spinach is wilted. Stir in the Italian seasoning and crushed red pepper flakes. Remove from the heat.

4. In a medium bowl, whisk together the marinara, cottage cheese, pesto, eggs, salt and black pepper until thoroughly combined. Using tongs, toss the marinara and cooked spaghetti into the casserole dish with the sausage mixture until combined and spread into one layer. Top with the shredded mozzarella.

5. Bake 28-32 minutes or until set. Turn the oven to a broil for 2-3 minutes or until cheese is bubbly and lightly browned. Remove from the oven and let sit 5-10 minutes.

6. Cut into wedges and serve with freshly grated Parmesan and parsley (if using).

SNACKS

31. Baked Chicken Nuggets with Honey Mustard

Prep Time: 10-15 mins

Cook Time: 13-16 mins

Total Time: 23-31 mins

Yield: Serves 6

Ingredients

Chicken Nuggets:

- 1-pound boneless skinless chicken breast, cubed
- ¾ cup all-purpose flour
- 2 large eggs
- 1 tablespoon Silver Spring Foods Dijon Mustard
- 2 cups panko breadcrumbs
- 1 ½ teaspoons kosher or sea salt
- ½ teaspoon ground black pepper
- ½ teaspoon each onion and garlic powder

Honey Mustard:

- 3 tablespoons Silver Spring Foods Dijon Mustard
- 2 tablespoons honey

Instructions

1. Preheat the oven to 375 degrees. Fit a wire rack inside a baking sheet and coat with cooking spray. Set aside.

2. Spread the cubed chicken on a cutting board. Set up 3 bowls: one with the flour, one with the beaten egg and Dijon and one with the panko breadcrumbs. Sprinkle with chicken with salt and black pepper, then distribute the remaining salt and black pepper and onion and garlic powder into the bowls with the flour, egg mixture and breadcrumbs. Whisk each to combine.

3. Dip the cubed chicken, one at a time, into the flour, then the egg mixture, then the breadcrumbs and line on the prepared wire rack an inch apart. Repeat until ingredients are used up.

4. Coat the chicken nuggets with cooking spray. Bake 13-16 minutes or until tender are firm and internal temperature reaches 165 degrees. Let slightly cool.

5. In a small bowl, whisk together the Dijon and honey until combined. Serve with chicken nuggets for dipping.

32. Strawberry Basil Bruschetta

Prep Time: 10-15 mins

Cook Time: 0 mins

Total Time: 10-15 mins

Yield: Serves 8

Ingredients

Crostinis:

- 10.5-ounce baguette, sliced ½-inch thick
- 2 tablespoons olive oil
- ¼ teaspoon coarse salt

Bruschetta:

- 1-pound strawberries, trimmed and diced
- 1 tablespoon olive oil
- 1 tablespoon honey or granulated sugar
- ½ tablespoon balsamic vinegar
- ¼ teaspoon coarse salt
- 4 ounces fresh goat cheese, ricotta or burrata
- Freshly cracked black pepper, to taste
- ½ cup fresh basil leaves, chiffonade

Instructions

1. Preheat the oven to 350 degrees. Line the baguette slices on a baking sheet and drizzle with olive oil. Sprinkle with salt. Bake 8-10 minutes or until lightly browned and crisp. Set aside to cool.

2. In a medium bowl, stir together the strawberries, olive oil, honey, balsamic and salt until combined.

3. Smear the goat cheese, ricotta or burrata on each baguette. Top each with a scoop of the strawberry mixture and a smattering of freshly cracked black pepper, then garnish with basil leaves. Serve.

33. Mini Chocolate Chip Muffins

Prep Time: 5-10 mins

Cook Time: 10-15 mins

Total Time: 15-25 mins

Yield: Makes 24 mini muffins

Method: Baking

Ingredients

- ½ cup whole wheat or whole wheat pastry flour
- ½ cup all-purpose flour
- 1 teaspoon baking powder
- ¼ teaspoon coarse salt
- ⅓ cup granulated sugar
- ¼ cup oil
- 1 large egg
- 1 ½ teaspoons pure vanilla extract
- ¼ teaspoon pure almond extract (optional)
- ¼ cup plain or vanilla Greek yogurt
- ¼ cup milk
- ¼ cup mini dark or semisweet chocolate chips

Instructions

1. Preheat the oven to 350 degrees. Line a 24-cup mini muffin tin with mini muffin liners. Set aside.

2. In a medium mixing bowl, whisk together the flours, baking powder and salt until combined. In a separate medium mixing bowl, whisk together the sugar, oil and egg vigorously until mixture is fluffy and pale. Whisk in the vanilla extract, almond extract (if using), yogurt and milk until incorporated.

3. Pour wet ingredients into the bowl with the dry ingredients and fold until just incorporated. Fold in the chocolate chips.

4. Use two spoons to scoop mixture into mini muffin tin wells. Bake 9-13 minutes or until just set. Let cool before serving.

34. Coconut Date Energy Bites

Prep Time: 10 min

Cook Time: 0 min

Total Time: 10 min

Yield: Makes 15 bites

Ingredients

- 12 pitted Medjool dates
- ½ cup unsweetened shredded coconut
- ½ cup chopped walnuts or almonds
- 1 ½ tablespoons melted coconut oil

Instructions

1. Place all the ingredients in a food processor and pulse until the mixture becomes a paste.
2. Form 2-inch bites, place in an airtight container, and store in the refrigerator for up to 2 weeks.

35. Lemon Poppy Seed Zucchini Muffins

Prep Time: 15 min

Cook Time: 25 min

Total Time: 40 min

Yield: 12 muffins

Ingredients

- 1 cup whole wheat pastry flour*
- 1 cup old-fashioned rolled oats
- 2 tablespoons ground flax seed
- 2 teaspoons baking powder
- ½ teaspoon coarse salt
- 2 large eggs
- 6-ounces plain or vanilla Greek yogurt (about ⅔ cup)
- ½ cup granulated sugar
- 3 tablespoons oil
- 1 teaspoon pure vanilla extract
- 1 teaspoon pure lemon extract (optional)
- 1 medium zucchini, shredded (about 1 ½ cups)
- Zest and juice of 1 medium lemon (about ¼ cup)
- 1 ½ tablespoons poppy seeds

Instructions

1. Preheat oven to 350 degrees. Prepare 12-cup muffin tin with muffin liners.

2. In a medium mixing bowl, which together flour, oats, flax, baking powder and salt until combined.

3. In a separate medium mixing bowl, whisk together eggs and sugar until fluffy. Whisk in yogurt, oil, vanilla extract and lemon extract (if using) until combined. Stir in shredded zucchini, lemon zest and juice and poppy seeds.

4. Fold dry ingredients into the bowl with the wet ingredients and mix until just combined.

5. Scoop muffin batter into the prepared muffin cups, filling about ¾ of the way to the top. Bake 22-27 minutes or until muffins are just set. Allow to cool on a wire rack.

36. Beet Hummus

Prep Time: 15 min

Cook Time: 0 min

Total Time: 15 min

Yield: Serves 8

Ingredients

- 2 cups cooked whole beets
- 1 (15-ounce) can garbanzo beans, rinsed and drained
- Zest and juice of 1 medium lemon
- ¼ cup tahini (sesame seed paste)
- ½ teaspoon coarse salt
- ½ teaspoon ground black pepper
- ½ teaspoon ground cloves
- ¼ teaspoon cayenne pepper
- ¼ cup olive oil
- Pita bread or chips, for serving

Instructions

1. Place beets, garbanzo beans, lemon zest and juice, tahini, salt, black pepper, cloves and cayenne in the bowl of a food processor. Puree while drizzling in the

olive oil through the vegetable shoot until smooth, scraping the sides as necessary.

2. Taste and adjust seasoning, if necessary. Serve with pita bread or chips.

37. Oat, Coconut & Walnut Bars

Prep Time: 10 min

Cook Time: 0 min

Total Time: 10 min

Yield: Makes 12 bars

Method: No-cook

Ingredients

- 1 (7-ounce) package Mariani Probiotic Pitted Prunes
- 2 cups old-fashioned rolled oats
- 1 cup unsweetened coconut flakes
- ½ cup chopped walnuts
- 3–4 tablespoons honey
- 3–4 tablespoons melted coconut oil
- 1 tablespoon chia seeds

Instructions

1. Line a 9×9 baking dish with parchment paper.
2. Place all ingredients in the bowl of a food processor and pulse until a sticky dough forms. Transfer dough to the parchment-lined dish and press evenly into a square. Refrigerate at least 2 hours.
3. Lift the bars out of the baking dish using the edges of the parchment paper and place on a cutting board.

Cut into 12 bars. Store in the refrigerator in an airtight container or bag.

38. Mini Peanut Butter & Jelly Dark Chocolate Cups

Prep Time: 20 mins

Cook Time: 5 mins

Total Time: 25 mins + refrigeration time

Yield: 48 Cups

Ingredients

- 2 (16-ounce) bag dark chocolate chips
- ½ cup coconut oil or butter, divided
- 1 cup natural creamy peanut butter
- ½ cup powdered sugar (or Swerve Confectioners')
- ¼ cup strawberry preserves

Instructions

1. Line two 24-cup mini muffin tins with mini muffin liners.
2. Microwave dark chocolate chips and ¼ cup coconut oil or butter in a glass bowl at 30 second increments, stirring in between increments, until melted (usually takes 2 minute or 2 minutes 30 seconds).
3. In another glass bowl, microwave remaining ¼ cup coconut oil or butter and peanut butter for 1 minute. Add the powdered sugar and whisk to combine.

4. Spoon about ½ tablespoon chocolate mixture into each mini muffin liner, then about ½ tablespoon peanut butter mixture, then a drop of strawberry preserves, finishing with another ½ tablespoon chocolate mixture. In between each layer, gently pick up and drop the muffin tin onto the counter or gently shake the pan to flatten each layer.

5. Place in the refrigerator for at least 30 minutes, until hardened. Keep refrigerated in an airtight container.

39. Crock Pot Apple Fritter Bread

Prep Time: 15 mins

Cook Time: 2 hrs

Total Time: 2 hrs 15 mins

Yield: Serves 12

Ingredients

- 0.25-ounce package active dry yeast (about 2 ¼ teaspoons)
- 1 tablespoon honey
- 1 ¼ cups warm water
- 1 ½ teaspoons coarse salt
- 3 cups whole wheat pastry flour + a few spoonfuls
- 2 tablespoons ground flax seed (optional)
- 3 medium sweet apples, diced
- ½ cup walnuts, chopped
- 2 tablespoons butter, melted
- 1 ½ teaspoons cinnamon
- 2 tablespoons brown sugar

Instructions

1. Place yeast, honey and warm water in the bowl of a stand mixer. Whisk to combine. Allow to sit for 15-20 minutes, until mixture has puffed up.

2. Fit mixer with dough hook. Stir in salt, then mix in flour, ½ cup at a time, with the mixer running on low. Mix in flax seed, if using. Allow dough to mix on low for 4-5 minutes, until a ball has formed. Dough should be slightly sticky. Mix in diced apple and walnuts until combined.

3. Place a few spoonfuls of flour on a large piece of parchment paper. Transfer dough to the paper and form a ball. Place a damp cloth over the dough and allow to rise for about 1 hour or until dough has doubled in size. Transfer dough with the parchment paper into the crock pot. Set on low.

4. Whisk together melted butter, cinnamon and brown sugar in a liquid measuring cup. Pour mixture over dough and swirl it into the dough with a butter knife. Place the lid on the crock pot and allow to cook for 1 to 2 hours, until internal temperature of bread reaches 190-200 degrees.

40. Frozen Chocolate Banana Pops

Prep Time: 15-20 mins

Cook Time: 0 mins

Total Time: 15-20 mins + 2 hrs freezer time

Yield: Makes 8 bananas

Ingredients

- 8 small bananas, peeled
- 8-ounces chocolate chips
- Toppings: Sprinkles, coconut, salted nuts, pretzels, mini marshmallows, chopped fruit, sea salt, caramel, melted peanut butter, etc.

Instructions

1. Skewer the bananas using a wooden kebab skewer, leaving enough sticking out to use as a handle.
2. Place a large piece of parchment paper on a cookie sheet.
3. Heat dark chocolate chips in a double boiler or microwave, stirring every 30 seconds, until melted.
4. Dip bananas into the melted chocolate, using a spoon to evenly coat the bananas with chocolate. Place the banana on parchment paper.

5. Immediately cover the banana with toppings of your choice. Place in the freezer for at least 2 hours.

www.ingramcontent.com/pod-product-compliance
Lightning Source LLC
LaVergne TN
LVHW012346170525
811580LV00010B/562